The Joy of
Friendship

The Joy of Friendship

A celebration of life, laughter, and lasting memories

Lois Blyth

CICO BOOKS

LONDON NEW YORK

Friendship is ...
The hand that steadies
The eyes that never turn away
The ears that listen
One who knows when to go
and when to stay.

Lois Blyth

Published in 2014 by CICO Books
an imprint of Ryland Peters & Small Ltd
20–21 Jockey's Fields, London WC1R 4BW

www.rylandpeters.com

10 9 8 7 6 5 4 3 2 1

A CIP catalogue record for this book is available from the British Library.

ISBN: 978-1-78249-108-8

Printed in China

Editor: Marion Paull
Designer: Emily Breen
Illustrator: Amy Louise Evans

For digital editions, visit www.cicobooks.com/apps.php

Contents

Preface

When writing a book on happiness a few years ago, I was surprised to find myself writing first about unhappiness—how to get out of your own way, so that you can open yourself up to happiness. In writing about friendship, something similar happened. To celebrate the joy of friendship all you really need is the willingness to connect to people, to spend time and share experiences with them, and a scrapbook or Facebook account to record your memories. But to find friends, receive friendship, and to *be* a friend, you first need to believe that you are worthy of friendship, and that you have something about you that other people value. Perhaps to truly appreciate friendship we need to also understand loneliness, and know what it is like to be on the outside looking in.

Friendship is a continuation of kinship. It is less about popularity or the number of connections we have gathered online, and more about how we connect, and our thoughts, actions, and feelings toward other human beings in our life. Friendship provides a sense of belonging that motivates us to care for people, to be willing to give of ourselves and make time for others—even when it is inconvenient. We may need to become stronger, more vulnerable, or more willing to compromise than we would naturally choose in order to develop friendship, but the rewards are always worth it.

Our capacity for friendship has the power to change our world. It transforms into shared memory and is the glue that binds all of us together. It is the partner of forgiveness, reconciliation, and healing—as well as of companionship, joy, and fun. Our bonds of friendship are some of the most precious we have, because they are life-changing and life-enhancing, and they can help us to become the best we can be.

Introduction

Everyone needs friends. They are the people who understand how we think, who challenge us, and whose opinions we value. Our friends are the people with whom we want to share the good times, and who we miss when they are not around. They make life fun and they make us laugh. They help to shape our lives and our memories.

During the tough times, friends become the wall of comfort that protects us from loneliness; they are the scaffolding that holds us up when we are in danger of falling; they are the support network that encourages us to reach for greater heights when we doubt our ability to succeed. They act as a mirror that reminds us who we truly are. Friends are the people who are there for us when life doesn't turn out quite as planned, and we are more than happy to be there for them, too.

Never before have so many people had so many friends. In an instant we can click, tweet, follow, connect, and befriend almost anyone, anywhere. But what does it take to be a friend? What are the qualities of enduring friendship? How can you be a better friend to others, while also remaining true to yourself?

> When you make time for your friends,
> you make time for life.

Lois Blyth

The *Joy of Friendship* is a celebration of connectedness and a tribute to those who enrich our lives with their support, strength, and laughter. It reflects upon the changing nature of friendship through the years, the power of sustained friendships, and the important part that our buddies,

friends, peers, and acquaintances play throughout every stage of our lives. It is written as a gift that one friend might give to another, in appreciation for who that person is—and all they mean to us.

Friendship is ...
... always starting from where you left off.
... sharing a unique bond that no one can break.
... sharing memories that will live on forever.
... feeling a whole and valued person.
... letting go of all inhibitions and laughing
at silly things.
... being able to share personal thoughts
without being judged.
... feeling young again and never growing old.
... enjoying quality time together.
... looking out for each other.
... as precious as peace of mind, which is so
often taken for granted.

Sue Lanson

1

THE PATH TO FRIENDSHIP

Friends are the family we
choose for ourselves.

Anon

How do we choose our friends?

Our friends mark the passage of our lives and help to define who we are. They are hard-wired into our memories of the past, our plans for the present, and our hopes for the future. When we think back, we remember not only what we have done, where we have been, and what we have achieved, but also what we felt, and who shared our  experiences with us. For better or worse, friends bear witness to our hopes, dreams, and fears, and all that transpires from the decisions we choose to make.

The roots of friendship can lie in the smallest gestures—a welcoming cup of coffee when you are moving into a new house; a reassuring comment when you are confused on your first day at school, college, or work; a listening ear when you are feeling distressed; a friendly invitation to join in, to make sure you feel one of the crowd. Friendship starts when someone reaches out, and shows that they are watching out for you, or have recognized that you have something in common.

We may think that we choose our friends for who *they* are, but psychologists believe that in reality we choose them because they validate who *we* are.

The law of similarity

When a group of strangers gathers together, the chances are we will be drawn initially toward the people with whom we are likely to have things in common.

The signals may be fairly superficial:
- A similar style of dress.
- Preference for a similar place in the room—near the back or in a quiet spot, for example; or at the front, in the throng.
- Early/late arrival; friendly/reserved attitude.
- The have children who look the same age as your own.

Or more subtle:
- A facial expression that echoes your own feelings.
- Familiar body language that conveys a recognizable message.
- A certain something that reminds you of someone who is already in your life—or vice versa.

Whatever the signs may be, if we find we would like to talk to a particular person, it's because we recognize them as being similar to ourselves or to someone we have met before, or as someone who just looks interesting.

The gift of humor

How often in your life have the seeds of friendship been sown via a shared sense of humor? Laughter brings people together in an instant. When people share a laugh, they show immediately that they share an understanding. Making people laugh and smile is a wonderful gift that turns a stranger into a possible friend. Choosing to turn an awkward situation into something amusing changes it from a potential disagreement to something that is of little importance.

The rule of fun

The first rule of thumb when making friends is that the person you are hanging out with needs to "get" who you are and be fun to be with. Of course, everyone's idea of fun is going to be different, but common ground will be there all the same.

"The first time I met my friend Freya, we were at an arty 'do' at a local gallery. She was a sculptor of some renown, who was also extremely tall and stylish. I was struck by how formidable she looked. When we were introduced, there was no welcoming smile (which I later realized was due to shyness) and I thought she was rather stand-offish. I have a tendency to cover up moments of discomfort by making very poor jokes, so I said something reasonably inane to break the ice. And she laughed—the kind of belly laugh that shows a love of life and a sense of fun. We clicked in that moment.

We are radically different people, but we share a slightly anarchic outlook on life. We have been friends ever since." **Anna**

The skill of empathy

Friends tend to share each other's joy and feel each other's pain; they empathize with one another. A friend's happiness can often lift our own spirits because they want us to share in the moment. Our empathy can also lead us to extend warmth and kindness, and show friendship to others who we don't yet know.

Empathy is a close friend of compassion. When disaster strikes, empathy and compassion motivate total strangers to help one another. We may not share another's emotions, but we can relate to how they must be feeling. Empathy and compassion lead to friendships being forged out of the depths of catastrophe or despair.

We are not born with feelings of empathy; it is a skill that we learn through our experiences in early life and as our brain develops. Without it, we find it harder to relate to other people and forge friendships. It is a vitally important part of being human (although anyone who has had a favorite pet would say that animals can show empathy, too).

The signs of trust

When we first start chatting to new people, we are usually trying to build bridges—to seek out points of similarity, even when the common ground sounds tenuous. "Oh, you're Italian? My best friend's father is Italian. I just love Italian people." (Okay, sometimes this instinct can be rather annoying.) But in those moments of reflection we also encourage the other person to disclose something about themselves.

Psychologists will often say that a friendship is defined by the level of shared disclosure. In other words, if I tell you about something that is going on in my life, will you take a risk and share something that is going on in yours with me? When we choose our friends we are asking: "Can I trust you with my secrets?"

Most of us learn at a very young age that a secret shared is a secret put under threat. There is no greater test of loyalty in friendship than sharing a confidence that you don't want to be disclosed to anyone else. Friendships (and relationships) can survive most things, but a breach of trust is often a contract breaker.

> "Katie is a wonderful friend but I am careful about what I say to her; she has told me too many things about other people over the years!" **Clare**

And therein lies the rub of course. We may try to protect ourselves (and others), but when we do, we put up barriers, too.

> "I never really get the sense that I know the real Clare. She can be good fun when she is in the right mood, but she doesn't open up very easily." **Katie**

To win friendship, we need to take risks and show others that we are willing to make ourselves vulnerable and put ourselves in their care.

The path of friendship

Generations of psychologists have spent years studying ways in which the bonds of friendship are formed, evolved, broken, and resolved. The depth and complexity of our friendships is connected to the development of the brain, which creates our memories and our sense of self. Somewhere along the line, our essential self develops a core that becomes our identity. Early friendships focus on "me and my wants"; later friendships are more concerned with "us and our needs". However, whatever age we are, we have to become aware of others' needs before we can learn to share, or put other people before ourselves.

Parents watch their children develop through four ages and stages as they learn to mix with others and make friends:

- Playing and sharing
- Helping and supporting
- Trusting and caring
- Making both independent and group friendships.

Hanging out—toddler style

The chances are we won't really remember playing with anyone at this age (although our early friends probably feature in the photos in the family album!). Tiny tots don't so much play together as play alongside one another. Playtime is toy time. Toddlers' attention spans are intense and short-lived, so petty scraps are fairly frequent as one small person takes a fancy to what another person has. Toddlers can be very physical. What's mine is definitely *"all mine"* at this age! Friendships last only for a few minutes or a few hours at a time, but that is not surprising since it is not until age three that the brain develops the ability to manage emotions. That is why small children find it hard to say sorry or to share. By age four most of us were on our way to making and keeping friends.

Playground pals—young friendships

Even if you don't remember your first day at school, the chances are you can remember how yo ufelt about some of the children, and the friends you made there. The school playground is where children learn to play together and get along with one another. Somewhere around four or five years old we started to learn that not everyone sees things in the same way we do, and friendships are based on who wants to play with me *now*!

Children can be very sharing, caring, and forgiving at this age, and have a strong sense of fair play. Young friends can invent and share a fantasy world that keeps them happy for hours. Their imaginations are in full flow and they can create their own environment in an instant. A chair may no longer be a chair, but a room in a playhouse; a plain cardboard box becomes a rocket ship or a submarine; a tree trunk is a store front. Friendships often revolve around doing things and making things happen.

By the time we were six, seven, or eight years old, we may have become more choosy about who we like and dislike, but we have usually learned what we need to do to get along with people and that sometimes we need to compromise. Generally speaking, the approach is: "If you are here and you are being nice, you are my friend!" and although friendships are changeable, children often stay friends for several weeks at a time.

> "I have very fond memories of my childhood. It was all about having fun. We didn't have a television and I seem to remember spending most of my childhood playing outdoors. Indoors was for meals and sleeping. Games played with friends revolved around the characters and ideas from adventures and mysteries we had read. We were forever looking for treasure, imagining strangers to be escaped robbers or spies, and creating secret 'dens' and hideaways where we could plot, scheme, and create neverending stories."
>
> **Karen**

Best friends forever—the pre-teen years

If you pass a group of friends aged somewhere from nine to thirteen, the chances are they will be giggling over a private joke and having fun. Once we start to make our own decisions about whether we like people, our friendships start to define who we are. Most of us learn to empathize with other people, know that we have to stand up for our friends, and for what is right. We know that we should be kind to other people, even if we don't really take

to them. Pre-teen friends can be very close and remain solid for months or years at a time. The chances are that you may barely remember what your friends looked like, but you will remember the things you did together. Childhood tends to be a blur of activity, accented by key events—whether good or bad. Children don't tend to be too interested in status, salary, or country of origin—they just care about having fun and getting along. Friendships are made in an instant and are based on geography—friends made in childhood tend to live close by, be roughly the same age, and are just willing and able to come and play.

BEST FRIENDS FOREVER

Did you have a best friend in elementary school or high school? Were they a BFF (Best Friend Forever) or did you prefer to have lots of friends rather than one in particular? Children and teenagers are experts in friendship. Friends can be made and lost in an afternoon; new ones can be forged on the strength of a shared joke, or the latest trend, but best friend status is something very precious indeed. Best friends have access to secrets. They know your vulnerabilities and have the patience to see you through the tough times. A best friend is expected to be fun, understanding, loyal, supportive, trustworthy—and should be willing to share shoes, clothes, secrets, or relationship advice at a moment's notice. We may have more than one best friend, and over time they will probably become our inner circle of friends. They are the ones we want to share the good times with, the landmark moments, as well as the challenges in life. They bring us joy when we see them and lift our spirits when we are down. Our best friends make our world a better place.

"I can remember my brothers and I used to become friends with other kids in an instant. Our summer holidays were spent touring and camping, and one of the first things we'd do once the tent-trailer was set up, was to wander around looking for other kids our age to kick a ball around, play frisbee or come with us to find somewhere to buy a soda. We would size each other up a bit but as far as I can remember, we always used to end up getting along. Life always seemed carefree and simple at that age."

Ricky

A parallel universe—teenage friends

Teenage friendships can be very intense, and very loyal. Many teenagers spend more time with their friends than they do with their parents and will confide in them about their fears, worries, and dreams. Many of us will remember our teenage years as a time of feeling separate from parents and family. We may live under the same roof, and really care about our family, but most of our time is spent focused on our friends and relationships at school. We want to fit in with a particular crowd, hang out with our friends, and try to make peace with our self-consciousness and imperfections. Friends may be left out, picked on, or dropped dramatically, but friendships made at this age can also last for life. It is the age when having friends really matters—when hormones start to play their part, and when the person you like is guaranteed to fall for your best friend!

"When my family moved house toward the end of my time in Junior High, I was completely devastated. My friends were my world. On the day that everyone else was getting ready for the end of year Prom, I was traveling behind a removal truck and feeling anxious about starting at a new school in the fall. My best friend Beth had come to see me off that day and had given me a gift. It was a wall banner covered in drawings and little rhymes that she had created herself. It hung on my wall all through my teens. Recently, when I was clearing out my attic, I found it again, wrapped up in a storage tube. The memories of thirty years ago came flooding back and I just cried! I was right back there, trying to be brave at twelve years old and reading all the messages for the first time." **Millie**

"I grew up during the era of glam rock and punk rock, so the photos of my friends and me aged fifteen are completely outrageous! It didn't occur to us that the music or the fashions would change. At that age you assume that the world as you know it will be unchanged forever!" **Tom**

The world is my friend—twenties plus

Many teenagers leave their neighborhood when they leave school, and head off to work or college in other regions or towns. This coming of age is a time of independence and personal discovery. Deeper friendships evolve as we try to become more adventurous, push the boundaries of our upbringing, and try to discover who we are. These are the friends who mark our independence and who may influence our life decisions and choices.

"I thought I knew exactly who I was when I was twenty-one. I had it all worked out: who my friends were, what I liked, what my opinions were. My life was set and I was super-confident about what I would achieve. I was right about one thing: several of my friends are still my friends! They have stuck with me, but the rest has evolved and changed." **David**

Looking back—in older age

The joy of childhood friendships is that they never really leave us. We may not have seen someone for twenty, thirty, or forty-plus years, but if we knew them when we were school-aged, the deep knowing of that person is still there. We are never so very far from the school playground. Throughout life we are looking for people with whom we can hang out and have fun, who will understand us.

The enjoyment of adult friendships is the freedom to be honest with one another. We know that the world is not perfect and neither are we. Getting together, or talking, is as much about reassuring ourselves that we are okay as we are, as it is about trying to improve and do things better.

Maria grew up in a small town in the south of England; she and her friends went all through school together. She still takes a week off to go away with her four closest friends every year, even though they are now spread all around the globe. "It feels as if nothing has changed," she says. "The second we are back together the years melt away, and we laugh from the moment we meet until the moment we say goodbye. We have made very different choices in life, but we have a deep understanding of one another that will never go away. I know that in a true crisis they would always be there for me."

Don't walk behind me; I may not lead. Don't walk in front of me; I may not follow. Just walk beside me and be my friend.

Albert Camus (1913–60)

2

THE ART
OF GIVING

The only way to have a friend
is to be one.

Ralph Waldo Emerson (1803–82)

Give and take

Friendship is not about me or you, it's about us. Friendship grows out of the energy that two or more people create when they are together, and it thrives when a friend puts the needs of another before his or her own. But for a friendship to be sustained, the energy has to be balanced. There needs to be give, as well as take, on all sides. That may seem an obvious thing to say, but sometimes it doesn't quite work out that way. Sometimes, when life becomes very busy, or our own challenges take up all our time and energy, we may become preoccupied. Suddenly, we realize that we are out of touch, or have stopped asking what is happening in other people's lives.

The gift of time

Friendships, like plants, will flourish in a place of care, but will eventually wither when neglected. The strongest friendships are unlikely to die, however. Instead, they lie dormant, waiting for the right moment to burst back into life. For a friendship to survive and grow, it needs time and attention—things that seem to be in shorter supply the older we get.

Five common obstacles lie in the way of reviving a valued friendship, but they can be overcome:

- Too busy to see anyone? Put a date in the diary anyway. One of the reasons we lose touch is everyday busyness; we keep putting it off.

- Is money tight? Meet for a walk, go to a gallery, or take a picnic instead of meeting for dinner or a drink.
- Do your partners clash? Then go solo and meet your friend on their own.
- Not sure what to say after so long? Stop worrying and just pick up the phone for a chat in the old-fashioned way. Nothing is better than the human voice, apart from seeing someone in person.
- Worried that you are less successful, less fit, more overweight, less interesting than you used to be or they are? The chances are they won't notice your insecurities unless you point them out—and if they are true friends, they will be concerned and want to reassure you anyway.

Figure out the real reason why you have not been in touch for so long. Perhaps there are issues surrounding money, choice of partner, children, schools, or differences of opinion? Could you be letting something relatively trivial get in the way of holding on to something precious? Sometimes we put obstacles that others are experiencing in our own way, too. However, our friends are often the very people who can help us to break free of our troubles and start striding forward again.

Tokens and symbols

As someone once said, "Friendship is not one big thing, it is a million little things." That is so true; it is a million acts of kindness, words of care, both spoken and unspoken. Sometimes, on birthdays and special holidays, we also enjoy swapping tokens of friendship, to show how much we care about one another.

When we have to say goodbye or spend time apart, a gift can act as a symbolic token of connection that helps to keep the memory of a dear friend close to mind.

Gifts, tokens, and symbols of

FRIENDSHIP DOLLS

In 1927, Dr Sidney Gulick of the Committee of World Friendship among Children, arranged for 12,739 blue-eyed American friendship dolls to be sent to Japanese children, as a gesture of goodwill and to encourage international understanding and friendship. In exchange, 58 beautifully-produced and individually unique dolls, dressed in kimonos, were sent from Japan to libraries and museums across the USA. Parties were thrown for the dolls and they were transported miles around the world as goodwill ambassadors for both countries.

friendship have been exchanged for as long as mankind has been on the planet. Having physical reminders of the people we care about helps to keep us connected across miles and years. From decorated stones and chains of beads to elaborate rings and expensive watches, friends, family, and lovers have always exchanged tokens of affection and reminders of precious moments together.

Photographs

How many hundreds and thousands of photos are taken and posted online each year? How many albums of prints from years gone by offer comfort and interest to those who browse through them? Before the first camera was invented, portrait painters perfected their art and created miniature pictures for loved ones to carry in lockets or pocket watches. When we can't have the real thing, looking at an image of someone we care about is enough to trigger memories and bring them to mind.

"My great friend Susan is wonderfully well organized, and each year she creates an enormous collage of photos from key events that have happened during the year, which she then puts on the wall. Her children love them, and have grown up surrounded by images of their childhood. Something that began as a bit of fun has become a chronicle of their family life."

Grace

Coco is a student in London, England. Her family lives in Rio de Janiero, Brazil, and her bedroom walls are covered with so many photographs there is no wall to be seen. "I am happy at college," she says, "but at the same time, I miss them so much. Looking up at their smiling faces stops me from feeling lonely—and I talk to their pictures every day!"

Rather than tucking your photos away in albums, consider getting prints of your favorite images and putting them up on your walls.

Cards and letters

There is something quietly exciting about hearing the dull thud of a greetings card landing on the doormat, or receiving a handwritten envelope in the mail. Those of us of a certain age are probably still likely to send a card or a letter if we want to say something important or a lasting thank you, although letter-writing in the sense of keeping up a correspondence is probably a dying art. Some old-fashioned ways to make sure your friends feel cared for:

- Remember birthdays. Don't just phone, send a birthday card that can be savored, displayed, and treasured.
- Send postcards. You don't need to go on vacation to send a postcard. It's fun to send them with a short note, day to day.
- Write a "real" letter. Why not take the time to send a handwritten note to a relative or a friend? It is as much of a keepsake as a gift, and possibly more precious.

WAIT A MINUTE MR POSTMAN

Around 1916, an elderly man suggested to J.C. Hall, the founder of Hallmark cards, that it would be a good idea to produce a card that included a line of text, suitable for sending to friends. His suggestion was: "I'd like to be the sort of friend that you have been to me." It was a quote from a poem about friendship by "the people's poet" Edgar A. Guest. When the card became an instant best-seller (continuing to sell well for 70 years) it began a whole new approach to greetings cards. By 1919, Hall had introduced a range of cards to encourage the custom of sending them to show friendship, gratitude, and general thoughtfulness.

NATIONAL FRIENDSHIP DAY

In 1935, the United States Congress proclaimed the first Sunday in August National Friendship Day. The year-round exchange of friendship cards picked up in the late 1950s and rapidly gained in popularity during the '60s and '70s and remains popular today.

In the digital age, few people send written letters to their friends any more, but it is wonderful when someone takes a moment to send a card—or an SMS or an email—to say hello, or thank you, or that they are thinking of you.

"My elderly mother is still meticulous about writing to her friends regularly. She finds it so hard to hold a pen, but there is nothing wrong with her mind. She loves to send and receive letters, and still swaps recipes and news cuttings with her friends."

Peter

"My friend Mike has reminded me that I used to give him a very hard time when he started typing his letters to me, rather than hand-writing them. It used to feel so impersonal. How things have changed!"

Louise

E-gifts and greetings

Missing the post is no longer an excuse for missing special occasions. Online diaries and digital card services make it easy—in theory—to send special messages on the right day. For the majority of people, the easiest way to send a card or letter these days is online. Contemporary ways to stay in touch and feel connected:

- Send a digital greeting. Animated e-cards or personalized messages and videos are a great way to keep connected and bring people together, across the globe and across generations. There are digital advent calendars available too.
- Create a Facebook page for friends and family, but don't forget to use the privacy controls so that you limit who else has access to your news and photos.
- Keep your head in the clouds. Share your holiday photos by email or SMS via cloud storage, without having to worry about file size. (A digital photoframe is a wonderful gift for someone who doesn't have a computer and would like to share your photos.)

> "I use my Facebook page to keep in touch with everyone. Why put things in an album where you'll never look at them again? I love looking back over everything I have done with my friends."

K tty

Friendship bracelets

Often braided or woven, and very colorful, these are modeled on tokens of friendship that were exchanged by Aboriginal peoples in North America and other countries. The wearer is meant to honor the work that went into making them, and the person who presented the gift, by wearing them until the threads wear out and break.

Friendship rings

These take many forms. Some are interlinked strands that can be put back together in just one way, while others show interlinked hands. The Irish Claddagh ring features two hands (representing friendship) holding a heart (representing love), with a crown on top of it (representing loyalty.) When worn on the right hand, with the point of the crown toward the fingertips, the ring symbolizes friendship and the search for love.

Lapis lazuli

This beautiful blue gemstone is used in pendants, necklaces, and earrings as a symbol of friendship and universal truth.

Flowers

The language of flowers dates back as far as the Ottoman empire, but was especially popular in Europe during the Victorian era. Yellow roses and pear blossom are symbols of friendship; joy is expressed in a bouquet of red and yellow roses, or of delphiniums or gardenia; elderflower is the symbol of compassion. These days, however all flowers are warmly given and received by friends, whether as a simple posy or a large bouquet. Break with tradition; men enjoy flowers, too.

"My lovely neighbor was in her eighties, but she would always insist on looking after my cat and keeping an eye on my cottage when I was away, which was quite often. She became a wonderful friend, and she loved her garden. Each time I came home I found a tiny pitcher of freshly cut flowers on my kitchen table. It was a symbol of friendship that made me feel very cared for. Nasturtiums were a great favorite, and I always think of her when they come into bloom each year."

Carole

Gifts of food

A special place in our hearts (as well as our stomachs) is reserved for presents of food—especially if the gift is home-made. There is nothing nicer than receiving a home-baked cake or sharing a meal that has been prepared by a friend. Here are some ideas.

- Try half-dipping individual soft fruits into melted chocolate and leaving them on wax paper to chil. Then put them in petits fours cases to give away as gifts.
- Wrap home-made cookies in muslin bags, tied with ribbon.
- Make up a mini hamper with a cheese selection, or local produce, to give someone as a personalized present.
- Too busy to cook? Write out your favorite cake recipe and make up a DIY packet with all the ingredients ready-measured.

"One of the most fabulous meals I ever enjoyed was a simple plate of wild mushrooms on toast that my friend had foraged that morning from the heath close to where he lived. Apparently, the Czechs are crazy about mushrooms, and he knew which ones were safe to eat. His enthusiasm was so contagious, it sealed our friendship. (There may have been a little alcohol involved, too.) It was a wonderfully joyful meal that I will never forget!"

Rcs

INTRODUCING HERMAN—
THE FRIENDSHIP CAKE

Hermans are friendship cakes (Freundschaftskuchen) with a sourdough base known as a "starter." Once the sourdough has risen, it is divided up and passed on, from friend to friend and household to household, rather like an edible friendship letter. The tradition seems comes from Germany, and may be a variation of Friendship Bread, which originated in the Amish community as a way of ensuring that no one ever went hungry. In its modern-day, more lavish, form the sourdough starter's recipients can turn it into a whole variety of cakes, breads, and muffins.

If you would like to start your own Herman, here's how to do it.

1 packet of active dry yeast
¼ cup/60 ml/2 fl oz warm water
1 cup/150g/5 oz all-purpose/plain flour
1 cup/225g/8 oz superfine/caster sugar
1 cup/240 ml/8 fl. oz. warm milk

• Dissolve the yeast in warm water and leave for 10 minutes. Stir.
• Add the flour and sugar to the yeast, mixing together.
• Slowly stir in the warm milk.
• Cover the bowl with a clean cloth (a dishtowel will do) and leave at room temperature for 24 hours.

When the sourdough mix has risen, you can either use it, or follow a ten-day "grow your own Herman" plan, which involves stirring the mix daily, and on the fifth and ninth days adding a further cup of sugar, flour, and milk. It will begin to bubble and slurp and will also smell rather strange, owing to the action of the yeast in the mix.

By the tenth day, the dough will have quadrupled in size, at which point it can be divided into four. Traditionally, three of the sections are passed on to friends for them to use as starters for their own Herman, but they can also be frozen. You keep the fourth section. In theory, the "cake" can carry on being grown and multiplied indefinitely—although, as in the long tradition of all chain letters, some people may be a little put off by the idea (and by its strongly yeasty smell,) and quietly throw it out!

A quick search for "friendship cake" online will take you to a Herman website or two, including one dedicated to Herman the German Friendship Cake, and a community of devotees, who provide recipes and outline the steps in great detail. Many other recipes are available online, which will give you ideas on how to bake with your sourdough starter.

"A friend who I hadn't heard from in years called me for a chat and we were regretting that we lived too far apart to meet up for a cup of tea and a catch-up. A day or so later a mystery parcel arrived at my door. Inside was a special "Afternoon tea" package, complete with loose tea, cake, and cookies in a cotton bag. Every time I enjoyed a slice of cake and a "cuppa" over the next few weeks I thought of my friend. My cat adopted the cotton bag as a favorite place to snooze, too."

Sarah

"My parents were great gardeners and visitors would always leave with either a posy of flowers or a gift of some home-grown produce, carefully packaged. I know how carefully those vegetables were produced, and their friends used to prepare and cook them with equal care. Somehow food always tastes better, and you feel more gratitude, when it has been home grown."

Louise

Giving to yourself

We all know someone who seems to spend all their time giving to others and being friends to those around them, but who doesn't make time for themselves. If you are one of those people, it is time to make a pledge to allow time for you and your needs. If you can't do it for yourself, do it for those who care about you, because the more you take care of yourself, the more energy you will have to support the important people in your life.

Book a haircut, decide to spend a weekend away, treat yourself to an afternoon off to read a book, listen to music, or go for a walk. Get the bike out and head for the hills. Whatever you need to do to retune your senses and tune in to your inner self, now is the time to do it.

Ask yourself, "Do I treat myself as well as I would treat a guest in my house?" The answer, sadly, for many of us is "No." We are far more generous with others than we are with our own selves.

David Pitonyak

The art of receiving

Of course, the other side of giving is receiving, and not everyone finds that quite as easy, especially if the gift is a godsend or extremely generous, or both. Receiving more than we believe we should, or being given something of monetary value that is greater than we can give in return, can make us feel uncomfortable. In order for things to seem right, we tend to seek balance. No one likes to feel beholden, even to a friend.

However, in those moments, ask yourself: "Am I putting my own need to feel comfortable ahead of their wish to give?" "Does my desire to pay them back diminish their generosity?" "Do I have something of value to offer in return, which money cannot buy?" "Is our friendship strong enough to play the long game, and to believe that the balance will be redressed at some point in years to come?" If the answer to any of those questions is "No," then there may be times when resisting a gift is the right decision for you. At other times, though, it may be a moment to recognize that the act of generosity has given you a glimpse into the soul of the person who has chosen to be your friend.

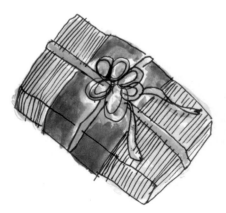

When Vicky moved house, her friend Penny offered to help her pack up and clear the house. On the day, she brought her boyfriend Tim with her, who Vicky had never met. "One part of me was embarrassed that Tim would be going through our things," remembers Vicky. "But he seemed a nice guy, and I was so desperate for help. My husband was away at the time, and unable to do anything. We had so much to get through, and so little time to do it in. I just had to swallow my pride and accept what was being offered. Tim was absolutely brilliant. He just mucked in and got on with things—and was pretty ruthless about throwing things away, too. I really needed that kind of focus and energy around me. I will never, ever forget such kindness."

"I was vacillating about whether or not to sell my house, but so many things needed fixing and upgrading, and I knew I wouldn't get them done without spending money that I didn't have. In an act of unbelievable generosity, my friend Nicole announced that she wanted to give me her old (by which think 'looks brand new') kitchen cabinets. Not only that, she was going to come and fit them. And there was no stopping her. She put in three days' hard labor and did it to perfection. My new kitchen looked so beautiful, I really didn't want to move! I felt overwhelming gratitude, but I felt incredibly uncomfortable, too. I had received more than I could possibly give in return. How could I ever repay her, or stop feeling beholden? I eventually realized that my feelings were all about me and not about her. I had to believe that, as she said, she really enjoyed being able to help. It really helped me to alter my perspective when another friend said to me, 'You know what? Life is long. There will be an opportunity to balance things out in the future.' Nicole assures me that she will not be afraid to ask when that time comes!"

Sarah

A lovely children's story explains the concept of love and friendship. It tells the tale of a village where everyone is happy. The children grow up believing in the idea of friendship tokens. Every time they offer a kindness to someone else, they also give them a friendship token. The more tokens they give away, the more they receive in return, so everyone is happy and everyone has a sense of belonging.

One day, a new child comes to the village, who hasn't got any friendship tokens. She feels miserable and an outsider, and resents the happiness that is going on all around her. She goes out of her way to discourage people from giving away their tokens. "Hang on to your tokens," she whispers. "Don't give them to her; you'll never get as many back in return." Over time, fewer tokens are in circulation and unhappiness and discontent begin to grow. No one really understands why.

One day, an elderly woman, who has seen a great deal of the world, notices that the girl seems discontented, and that every time she starts talking to people, they become unhappy. She gets chatting to the girl and asks her for some help carrying her large bag while they talk. The girl shrugs her shoulders and reluctantly takes the woman's bag. It feels very light, in spite of the size of the bag. "How very kind you are," the old woman says. "It was so lovely to meet you and spend time with you. I would like to give you some friendship

tokens. There are more here than I need. Please take these—and will you come back to see me tomorrow?" She reached into her bag, which was filled with tokens. And the little girl was filled with warmth and suddenly felt good about herself. She began to get a sense of belonging. On her way home she passed a boy who had fallen off his bike. "Let me help you up", she says, "and please have one of my friendship tokens." Which just goes to show that the more unhappy and lonely a person appears to be, the more they are in need of the gift of friendship.

Perhaps the greatest gift of all is the gift of our time and attention. There are times in every friendship when our friends don't seem to be themselves. They may be in pain, or angry, or they may try to push us away. These are the times when true friends remain steadfast—offering support and putting the needsof the other person before their own. Sometimes it requires patience and inner strength to remain a good friend, especially when someone is suffering or going through a difficult time. The cornerstones of friendship are honesty, humor, forgiveness, and acceptance. We may admire many of our friends and enjoy their company, but thoe we carry in our hearts and the ones we love exactly as they are.

No one can live a happy life if he turns everything to his own purpose. Live for others if you want to live for yourself.

Seneca (4BCE–65AD)

3

TUNING IN
TO NEW
FRIENDS

Depth of friendship does not
depend on length of acquaintance.

Rabindranath Tagore (1861–1941)

Building a network

We all have a need to be connected to other people. It is part of what makes us human. When we feel disconnected from others we also feel lost and vulnerable; we become disconnected from ourselves. Caring about others and having a network of friends is what gives our lives meaning and validation; it is part of our reason for being. More than one research project has shown that our happiness increases by a greater percentage when we are with our friends than when we are with our partners, children, or colleagues. Whether or not we care to admit it, we all need friends; they bring joy, love, humor, and a sense of belonging into our lives.

The need to belong

Connecting and belonging are slightly different things. Connecting is about reaching out and finding commonality and communion with other people; belonging is more deep rooted, coming from somewhere far deep within our being. It is related to place as well as person and has a grounding effect on who we are.

From the moment we learn to look beyond the limits of our family and toward the world outside, we start to make friends. There is a sense of recognition when we meet someone we feel we can connect to, and whose company we enjoy.

Overcoming obstacles
to making new friends

Venturing into the unknown to make new friends can leave many people feeling a little wobbly and insecure. No matter what age we are, facing a new stage in life without familiar friends around us can be a little daunting (and for some, downright terrifying.) It's rather like riding a bicycle for the first time without training wheels. You long to know that someone's running alongside, ready to grab you when you start to fall, but once you start pedaling and focus on the road ahead instead of the obstacles, the sense of freedom encourages your self-confidence and makes anything seem possible.

Meeting new people and making new friends is an opportunity for reinvention and self-discovery. As children and teenagers we fear that if we change school or move away, our old friends will forget us. Gradually we discover that while it is true that life goes on, there is always room in our hearts for both old and new friends.

Overcoming loneliness

Many people experience times in their life when they feel out of step with those around them, as if they are outside looking in. They are of the world, but not a part of it. Loneliness is a wall of pain and isolation that surrounds us during times of change and challenge. We may be in a crowded room, but feel a world apart; we may be surrounded by people but feel totally alone. When loneliness strikes it can feel as if the whole world has deserted us and we have no friends at all. Unfortunately, loneliness rarely travels alone, it often follows grief, and once it turns up, depression may be a bit too keen to knock on the door.

The wall of loneliness may feel impenetrable, but it can be knocked down in an instant. All too often, those people who say they don't have any friends actually mean that they don't believe they deserve friends or have anything to offer as a friend. They may be missing someone who is no longer in their lives, or who they have left behind. During times of loneliness it can take courage to reach out to other people, and patience too. Small steps may be all that can be managed to start with, but potential friends are everywhere; you just haven't met them yet.

There are several ways in which you might want to take the plunge to overcome loneliness:

- Volunteer to help with a charity that has some meaning for you. A lot of people resist this idea because they are worried they will be expected to commit more time than they can manage, but it doesn't have to be a heavy burden or a long-term arrangement. The magic is that the act of helping others and being appreciated can do wonders to alleviate loneliness.
- Go somewhere where there are like-minded people. Are you interested in music? Consider going to a local concert, and get chatting to someone during the interval. It only takes a smile and an appreciative comment to get a conversation started.
- Interested in sport? There are bound to be events in your area, and clubs are often looking for people to help out with coaching, general administration, or stewarding.
- Are books or writing your thing, or are you interested in taking up a language or learning a craft? There are likely to be reading groups or classes in your area.
- Too busy working to have time for making new friends? Focus on getting to know your work colleagues better, and find out how they manage to take time off at weekends.

The interesting thing is that when a group of complete strangers meets for the first time, and people are encouraged to start talking, the majority will find reasons to like each other, even if they felt reticent initially. Anyone who has ever attended a short training course, or joined a class, will know that once we get chatting to new people, we seem programed to find points of similarity. Even if we don't choose to take those relationships forward into the future, the seeds have been sown, should we choose to tend them.

'I find it a lot easier to get chatting to people who share my interests. Trying to hang out with other parents who we have met at the school gate, or dropping in to the local bar, just doesn't work for me. don't want to talk about myself or my family to people I don't know. I am a slow-burner when it comes to opening up or calling someone a friend."

Ryan

Overcoming shyness

Not everyone finds socializing easy. For many the barrier of shyness is so acute that it prevents them from knowing what to say or how to talk to people easily. But the "tools of the trade" are easy to learn. Once you are in conversation and focused on the other person, it will be easier to stop focusing on your worries and start being yourself.

Simple ways to keep shyness at bay:

- Smile and meet people's eyes when you say hello. When we are feeling tense or shy, there is a tendency to look down, cross our arms, or to frown. It is our instinctive way of becoming invisible or "taking flight." When we decide consciously to offer warmth, we are more likely to receive it in return. An old-fashioned handshake can help to connect you, mentally as well as physically, to the person you are talking to.

- When you first get talking, kick off by asking open questions that get the other person talking about themselves, and then pay close attention to what they say. It is the oldest strategy in the world, but it really does work. We may not remember what was said when we first met someone new, but we will remember how they made us feel.

- Some people find it useful to prepare things to say in advance, though others might find this only makes them worse, but a light-hearted ice-breaker about the weather, your journey, sport, or a current event is enough to gain an entry pass to a conversation.

- If you are more comfortable listening than talking, don't worry about it; there will be plenty of people willing to talk. The important thing is to be engaged, and not to look away, twitch, glare, or look bored!

The value of small talk

When we are surrounded by new people, we naturally try to seek out points of agreement or easy conversation, so we can feel comfortable in the situation and find our role within it. The most interesting points of connection are often hidden beneath the surface, so sometimes we need to navigate the small talk to get to a topic out of which something more engaging may arise.

Those who hate small talk and see it as superficial may find it useful to listen to what is being said in a different way. Even when people are talking about the weather, they are saying something about themselves. Some people moan, others are positive, someone else may joke about it. The topic itself is neutral and inoffensive, but in listening to the style and tone of people's banter, we understand more about those we have met.

If you are feeling nervous about entering a room full of people you don't know, take comfort in the fact that every other person in the room has felt the same way at some time, even (and sometimes especially) those who appear to be extremely extrovert. We all feel vulnerable in new situations. A person who is feeling shy is not the only one who is fearing judgment and rejection, and there is bound to be someone else in the room who is on the quiet side too.

When you are looking for a short-cut to fitting in, head straight for the person with the biggest smile who seems to know everyone already. The chances are they will be only too happy to introduce you and to make you feel at home. The great thing about extroverts is that they enjoy being around people. Far from pushing you away, if you approach them with a smile they will draw you into the fold, because an extrovert loves to connect people and to make things happen.

Facing up to a lack of confidence

Shyness and lack of confidence often go together, but whereas a shy person may be confident on the inside and ill-at-ease in social situations, a person who lacks confidence may feel that they have nothing to say and nothing to offer in comparison with others.

How to combat lack of confidence:

- Act as if you are confident. Walk tall, take deep breaths, relax your body, and think positive thoughts. The brain is easily persuaded, and will help you to become the confident person you want to be.
- Treat yourself to something that will lift your spirits and make you feel upbeat. Phone someone who will make you laugh or offer encouragement. Do whatever you need to do to make you feel good about yourself before you head into the arena.
- Focus on what other people are saying. The less you worry about yourself, the more genuinely interested you will become.
- Just get on with it. The more you ignore your fears and "jump in", the quicker you will get to know people, and your lack of confidence will fade.
- If your low confidence is holding you back in other areas of your life too, or if it is so debilitating that jumping in is out of the question, you may want to gather your courage and get some help from a professional therapist. Why put the rest of your life on hold when there are people around who can support you in understanding how to move on?

"I have always been lucky enough to have lots of friends and people assume I am naturally outgoing. Very few know how terrifying I find large social situations. I remember once, in my twenties, driving 87 miles to a party, which was a little nerve-wracking in itself, as I had only recently passed my test. I delayed leaving home because I was feeling anxious, which meant I arrived late. When I got there, I could see through the window that everything was in full swing. The room was packed with people and everyone seemed so together and sophisticated. I sat outside in the car for twenty minutes, willing myself to go in. But I just couldn't do it. I eventually turned around and drove all the way home again. I felt completely pathetic. My friend was not too impressed that I hadn't made it, either. I eventually confessed what had happened. She was incredibly sweet about it, and helped me to figure out a different way to approach things in the future. So these days, if I am on my own, I will plan to arrive when other people are arriving. It is much easier to chat to new people early on in the evening instead of halfway through. These days I don't let myself off the hook, either. If I have said 'yes', then I have to go. It is so rude otherwise. It took me a long time to realize that other people felt exactly the same way as I do. And it's just as well I found a way to overcome my fear, because I met my future husband at a party that I was tempted to wriggle out of going to!"

Lara

Life changes

Life happens. Relationships break down, we move house, change job, experience something life-altering, and for some reason our old friends and support network are not there any more. Very few people live or work in one place for long periods of time. The security of home is usually swapped for a new environment and new challenges. When we walk into a new environment for the first time, instead of seeing people as individuals, we may see a wall of strangers. In a new situation we may misinterpret a serious expression for disapproval, and someone's shyness for rejection. We may overanalyze our every move for fear of judgment. This can happen just as easily aged eighteen as it can at the age of eighty. In reality, most people are nice people—they just need time to get used to having someone new in their midst.

Starting afresh

Life can be challenging when we have too many changes at once; we may feel cut adrift and lose our sense of self for a while. The reality is that our true nature remains unchanged. By focusing outward, toward others instead of inward on our fears, something will shift in time.

I had a wonderful conversation with Charlotte, aged eleven, who was about to change schools. Bright, bubbly, and extremely positive, she was feeling uncharacteristically anxious about the new school year, because she wouldn't know anyone. Her parents knew, and I knew, that within a fortnight of arriving she was likely to have made new friends and be fitting in very happily—but in the meantime that was no help at all. The butterflies she was feeling in her stomach could almost be seen flying around the room. I felt for her, and remembered similar times in my own childhood, when moving house meant being the new girl once again.

However, Charlotte, like so many eleven-year-olds, is extremely wise. She told me that when new children attended her current school, they were partnered with a "buddy," who helped them to meet new people. One of her closest friends was a new girl who had been put under her own wing during the previous year. In her head, Charlotte knew already that she enjoys being sociable and gets along with most people. She would still be herself and would make new friends in time. Nevertheless, her journey into the unknown was not one she looked forward to.

Things don't really change that much as we get older. New social situations cause an element of anxiety; many people are nervous of change. The key is to be patient and to take small steps when entering a new environment.

Have you ever watched two animals circling and sniffing each other as they size one another up and decide whether they can share each other's territory? Humans are not so very different. We like familiarity. We take time to accept newcomers.

En masse we are creatures of habit, so things are shaken up slightly when someone new enters the fold.

You would think that the new person would be the one who is most uncomfortable with the situation, but, ironically, the people who are already in place are often the ones who feel under threat. Things are no longer as they expect them to be, so the new person is treated cautiously to begin with. Are they friend or foe? Will the newcomer threaten the status quo? We seek signs of safety and recognition to reduce the possibility of rejection when we first say hello. Our responses are no doubt rooted in some ancient instinct for survival, triggered when a stranger entered the village. Time and patience leads to acceptance.

The bridge of friendship

When we are feeling vulnerable, there is a tendency to worry about what others think and to assume everyone else is looking at us and judging us in some way. In reality, most of our anxieties are imaginary. The majority of people just want to feel liked, and will feel warm toward those who treat them in a friendly way. The fun of new friendships is getting to know people, and at the same time getting to know a new side to ourselves through that friendship.

However, for many people, making new friends can be stressful, especially if you are trying to break into an existing group, solo, or are changing lifestyle. No matter how many friends we have made over the years, or how confident we are in our own skin, moving to a new area or starting a new job or school can be daunting. Sometimes, the sense of being different or an outsider can be overwhelming. When that happens, there is no greater cure than inviting an existing friend or two to stay. It can be a lot more fun to explore a new place with someone else—and easier to get chatting to new people, too.

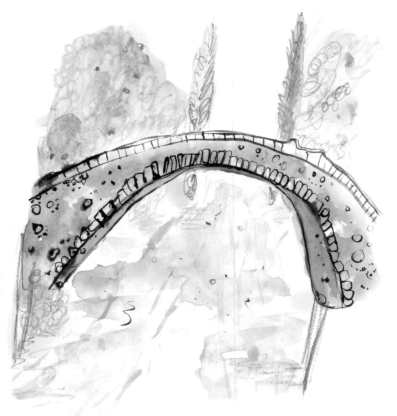

"I lost myself for a while. I had left a good job to relocate with my husband. He was working long hours to prove himself in his new role. For the first couple of months I felt completely adrift," says Anna. She invited two of her friends to visit one weekend and together they began to explore the local neighborhood. "It was great to relax and be myself again, and just have a laugh with people who know how I tick," she says. While they were having a coffee, one of Anna's friends got chatting to someone on the next table, who had dog. The woman turned out to be a neighbor of Anna's, and she invited Anna to walk the dog with her during the week. A friendship began, and Anna started to find her way into her new community. Her old friends were a catalyst for discovering new ones.

As the saying goes, strangers are new friends who you haven't met yet, but building friendships takes time. The path from acquaintance to friendship seems to get longer the older we are.

Making new friends is a little like a courtship. First we say hello and smile at a new acquaintance, introduce ourselves briefly, and form an initial impression. The next stage is often to talk a little when passing, and perhaps to mention something we are involved in or that interests us. If the other person shows an interest, too, there is an opening to get in touch or invite them to come along. If they resist, let it go, but try not to take it personally; there is most likely something else going on in their lives right now.

"I was going through a divorce and really didn't want to talk about it. I was very nervous of getting too close to new people because I thought they would want to know about my past. Eventually, I decided just to be honest, and tell them what was happening, but that I wasn't ready to talk about it yet. I wasn't intending to reject either them or their interest; it just wasn't helpful to me to dwell on it. I wanted to try to move on."

Belinda

"I know I come across as far too needy when I'm trying to make friends. I bake, I throw dinners, I give gifts. I want the whole world to be my friend! It took me a while to realize that some people feel smothered by that, until they get to know me and realize it's just the way I am!"

Anne

The friends we make in childhood have a unique understanding of who we are and where we came from. When we meet again in adult life, the years slip away and the deep knowledge of how each other ticks is still there, but we don't need to have known someone for years to recognize when we have met a kindred soul who understands us.

SPIRITUAL INFLUENCE

Do our spiritual beliefs influence the way we approach our friendships? How can they not? For those who follow the Buddhist approach to life, the idea of impermanence is central to their sense of connection. One friend from Singapore wrote to me about friendship :

"I have a few groups of friends that I divide my time with; religious friends, arty friends, travel friends, old classmate friends, new friends, and best friends. Due to my personality, I prefer to spend time with different groups as I believe each of them will broaden my knowledge and horizons. In life, things come and go, and because of the impermanence, I treasure what I have now. If you were to ask me whether friendship is forever, I can only give you a smile. To me, the most important person is the one I'm with, regardless if he or she is my best friend or new friend. I care and show appreciation to all my friends, thus this is how I define 'friendship'".

Vera

For others, the idea of impermanence is anathema. Some see their friends and friendship as rock solid and for life:

"For me, friendships are not to be taken lightly; they are very profound."

Christina

"I am very protective of my friends and would do all I could to make sure that they are not harmed in any way. When one of my closest friends told me she was getting married recently, I said to her fiancé, 'Don't you ever hurt her. If you do, you will have me to reckon with!' I think he was a bit shocked, and wasn't sure whether I was joking or not. I wasn't! She is a wonderful person and I wanted him to know that her friends expect him to treat her well!"

Holly

"Some years ago I was booked on a flight to London, England, from San Francisco, California. I love flying and like to reserve a window seat so I can enjoy every moment of the view. But this time I had checked in late and as a result was given a seat in the center of the middle aisle at the back of the plane. I was annoyed with myself. The last thing I wanted was to be sandwiched in between strangers for an eight-hour flight. I rummaged in my carry-on bag for a fat book to read to give me an excuse not to talk. But somehow it was never opened. The couple to my left were honeymooners, who wanted some tips on places to visit in London; they were charming. The person to my right was a very special lady, Mary. She noticed the title of my book and we started talking. We clicked immediately. She was a little younger than my mother and she had a daughter, who was a little younger than I am. Over the course of that flight we talked about everything and anything. In the process we somehow forged a friendship that has endured for years. We speak on the phone once in a blue moon, but every time we talk it is as if we have known each other forever."

Irene

Friendship is a slow-ripening fruit.

Aristotle (384–322BCE)

4

FRIENDS
FOR LIFE

Lots of people want to ride
with you in the limo. But what
you want is someone who will
take the bus with you when the
limo breaks down.

Oprah Winfrey

Keeping in touch

Have you ever had one of those moments when you have been thinking about someone just before that person called you, or just before you bumped into them in the street? (I once tripped over my best friend from primary school, literally, as she leant over to look at something on the bottom shelf in a store. We hadn't seen each other for ten or more years!) Have you ever found that someone you haven't thought about for a very long time is constantly coming into your mind—only to discover that something of great importance has been happening in their life, or that they have been thinking about you too?

For many people, close friends made in our younger years really do become friends for life. However, in a world where people move home, change job, and sometimes change country over time, it is all too easy to lose track of folk along the way, especially as growing families, work commitments, and other responsibilities start to play their part. As we get older, we may be left wondering: "How did that person slip out of my life? Where are they now?"

Beth lives in Toronto, Canada. She had a schoolfriend in childhood who had grown up in Scotland. They had been the best of friends in their early teens but had somehow lost contact over the years. One Friday afternoon on the way home from work, Beth noticed an advert for a Psychic Fair in her local mall. She was feeling a little restless and the tickets were half-price, so she laughed to herself that

it would be fun to see what they had to say. Among
the usual array of stalls offering astrological
predictions, crystal healing, and tarot readings, Beth
spotted a woman in her fifties with a gentle face,
who was sitting alone with her Labrador dog at her
feet. The notice above her head said she was a
psychic called Eileen. Not quite knowing why, Beth
approached her for a reading. "You will hear from
someone today who you have not spoken to for
many years," Eileen said. A likely story, thought Beth.
A half-hour later, as she turned the key in the door
of her apartment, she heard the phone ringing.
"Hello Beth," said a Scottish voice, "I came across
your home number when I was transferring details
to a new address book. I knew it was a long shot,
but I thought I would just give it a try. Your dad told
me how to reach you. How are you?"

The Universe really does work in mysterious ways. People come in
and out of our lives for a reason. Some of them will become lifelong
friends, and others are more of a challenge, but every encounter
shows us something new, helps us to learn something about ourselves,
and hopefully encourages us to offer support to one another.

Have you lost track of anyone important from your life? If you
took a moment to ask the Universe for assistance, you could be
surprised by the result. For those with less patience for such ideas,
there is always Facebook or Friends Reunited. Old friends may be just
a few clicks away.

WHERE ARE THEY NOW?

Fifteen years ago, Julia Pankhurst of Barnet, Hertfordshire in the UK, found herself wondering what had happened to her old schoolfriends and was inspired to set up a website to help reconnect people who wanted to get back in touch. With the help of a business partner, she and her husband launched Friends Reunited. By the end of the first year it had 3,000 members; by the end of year two, the site had grown to 2.5 million members. By year five, 15 million people had signed up to try to reconnect with old schoolfriends (and the site was sold for $208 million!). The average age of users is over forty. It seems that the older we get, the more likely we are to want to get back in touch with old friends.

Friends are good for our health—it's official

Meeting up with friends is uplifting and something to look forward to. When we meet with friends our cares slip away. We know that we are in safe company, can be our true selves, and can let go of our responsibilities for a while. Friends will listen to what we have to say (usually) without judgment, and care about us regardless of our mistakes (almost always), giving us time just to be ourselves.

Some people are very good at mixing their friends while others prefer to keep the different areas of their lives quite separate, but often at the core there will be a small group of people. These are the friends whom we can count on to make us laugh, and to listen to us. They will help us to think positively and look forward when the going gets tough. Even when we phase out for a while, it is easy to tune back in again the next time we're in contact.

When friends are happy, we share their joy; when they are suffering, we feel their pain and want to help. We share their emotions because in many ways it feels as if our friends are an extension of ourselves. Our lives are the richer for sharing time with them.

Friends are good for our health, too. Studies in the United States have shown that those with a strong social network are more likely to recover fully from a serious illness, probably because they feel loved and therefore feel they have more to live for. Those without friends are more likely to become homeless, destitute, or to develop addictions. It is a sobering thought.

Friendship and Kinship

In its purest sense, friendship is less about who we like and more about the all-inclusive nature of kinship. True friendship is about so much more than "you and me." It is about mutual support and human survival. As any soldier on the battlefield knows, a friend is someone who covers your back when you are facing grave danger. Friends stand together to face a common enemy, and would never leave one of their own kind to perish unaided.

Away from the battlefield, silent enemies can be equally life-threatening. Loneliness and isolation steal many lives. Feeling unsupported and unloved takes a toll on the body as well as the mind. Reaching out in friendship to those who seem alone, neglected, or in need is as necessary as breathing. If we turn our backs on those who need friendship and companionship the most, we turn our backs on our own humanity and the compassionate future of our own kind.

"Every winter for the last five years or so, an elderly man has returned to our small market town. It is impossible to tell exactly how old he is, but he is clearly living rough, and moves from place to place during the year. Last year we were especially concerned about him as the winter forecast was severe, so a local builder converted the annexe at the rear of our local church into a small flat. It included a kettle and a stove, a bed and a shower. We invited him to move in. He was quietly grateful, and stayed for two nights. By night three he was on the move again, perhaps feeling constrained by his new existence. Some people felt affronted, but he didn't mean to offend anyone! I'd like to hope he will be back again this year, knowing that he has a safe and warm place to stay should he need it."

Doc

"My friends are just amazing and I love them all dearly. I worry about them, too, and know that I turn into a mother hen when something is amiss in their lives. My boyfriend tells me I am the opposite of a fair-weather friend because I always turn up when dark clouds are gathering and someone is in trouble!"

Lucinda

"I am a Skype and Facetime addict. Once the children are asleep, I tend to settle down with a drink and give my mates in Oz a call to catch up on their day. I did the same when I was in hospital recently, so they met my nurses and one of the doctors, too! It was a scary time, and they were definitely the only people outside my family who I would have let see me covered in tubes and wearing a hospital gown. It was wonderful to have a giggle with them. They helped to take away some of my fear."

Mary

Some easy ways to show your friends that you care:

- Send a quick SMS to say hello. It never hurts to remind friends that they are important to you, and that you are thinking of them.
- Follow up on important news. It is all too easy to hang up the phone after talking, or read that text or email quickly, without making a note of the important events in your friend's life (the job interview/hospital appointment/son's audition) and before you know it, the moment passes. Don't leave your friend to follow up with you; be ready to ask first.
- Do something unexpected. If you have a friend who is overwhelmed by the needs of children and family, consider "cooking in" at their house, instead of eating out.
- Focus on fun. If you have a friend who is having a tough time at work or at home or who has health problems, encourage them to spend a whole day with you just having fun.
- Share the load. When someone is hosting an event/moving house/decorating/gardening, it makes things easier and more fun if friends help out to ensure things go smoothly.
- Stay alert. If one of your friends has gone quiet or is acting out of character, have the courage to ask what is really going on, even if it means receiving an evasive or defensive response.
- Share the limelight. If your friends have helped you to achieve a goal in life, don't forget to share the glory with them, too.
- Tell your friends they are fabulous. It's part of your job description!

Friendship milestones

When we are young, we find safety in numbers as we face life's challenges. We tend to talk about, and face up to, our "firsts" together—first boyfriend/girlfriend, first job interview, first job ... Whatever we are facing, we swap notes and discuss outcomes with our friends. There may be a few differences of opinion, changes of direction,

or spikes of rivalry here and there, but generally speaking we are all on the same road, bumping along and reaching the same place at more or less the same time.

Gradually, however, as time passes, the landscape changes. Our lives diverge and evolve at different paces, and we make individual choices about which path in life is right for us. Sometimes, the people we expected to journey alongside us, or be there for us, are nowhere to be found. At other times, we are surprised to find that friendships have weathered storms and lasted for years, without us noticing that the time has passed.

Our children, our friendships

Our children are one key marker of the passing of time. As adults we may kid ourselves that nothing has changed and that we are unchanged, but should we have them, children are witness to, and proof of, the passing years. Our lives form the foundations of their lives. Helping them to maintain healthy friendships often becomes more important to us than maintaining our own.

"My friends and I hadn't seen each other for over ten years. We were deep in conversation about old times in a "where has the time gone?" kind of way, trying to reassure ourselves that we were just as young and fabulous as ever, when the door burst open and their son bounded in from school. Suddenly, a symbol of the passing years was standing right in front of me. There was no overlooking his existence—he was now 6ft 2in tall!"

Eric

"The most precious gift ever given to me by my friends is the chance to be involved in the lives of their children. I have three godchildren and they all mean the world to me."

Ellie

Sometimes, however, we feel guilty, because instead of being joyful when we hear a good friend's news, we feel a tinge of jealousy instead. Parenthood can be especially challenging to friendships. At times, the role of friend and parent seem to conflict, especially when children are young.

"One of my dearest friends had invited a few people for drinks. All were mothers, apart from me. Part way through the evening she started to say that it was only by becoming a mother that a woman could fulfil her true purpose in life and that those who had not given birth could not truly know what it was to be female. It was totally unexpected. I felt as if she had dealt me a blow to my body. Not that she intended her comments for me, of course, but her maternal superiority knocked me sideways. It took me a while to calm my pain and jealousy."

Mathilde

"One of my closest friends had been trying to have a child via IVF for some years. Soon after I got together with my boyfriend I became pregnant. I had a real problem telling her my news. It seemed cruel after all she and her husband had been through, especially as I felt so unprepared for parenthood myself. Being the beautiful soul that she is, she now treats my son as if he were her own, and we have remained very close. She has never been able to have children, though."

Rachel

"My best friend and I drifted apart for a few years when our children were young, as our parenting styles turned out to be very different. She is a lawyer and had a nanny. She was all rules, regulations, and bedtimes, whereas I am embarrassed to say our house has always been a bit chaotic! Every time we met up she complained about something my children were doing. I started to feel guilty and also resented her comments. I'm ashamed to say I started to avoid her company. It was just easier that way. Fortunately, my kids have turned out to be quite well-adjusted, so I no longer feel I have to defend myself! My friend has become less rigid in her attitude, too, and our friendship is back on track these days. I think that's what having kids does for you!"

Moira

Some topics parents may like to avoid completely, unless asked about directly—and even then, approach with caution:

- Your opinion of your friend's children's school/behaviour/achievements/future prospects.
- Your own children's brilliance—especially if your friend's child has not done as well.

No matter how pleased your friend wants to be for you, the chances are they will be struggling with their inner lioness in defence of their young.

Of course, the majority of parents are mutually supportive for most of the time. They share trials and tribulations, life-balance challenges, and tips for a good night's sleep, and support each other when they choose to return to work. One universal rule of friendship always works, and heals all potential wounds—choose to put the needs of your friend before your own. If everyone were to follow that principle, every friend in the world would have their needs met fully. There would be no need to protect ourselves from hurt or disappointment at all.

Looking back

Personal friendships increase in importance as the years go by. Many of the older generation can begin to feel as if they are part of a world that no longer exists. Talking to others who share similar memories to their own can ward off melancholy and loneliness, and help people to cope with the struggles of growing old. Making friends with younger people can be an immense benefit, too. Very few older people feel the same age inside that they look on the outside. Feelings of aging are caused less by biological age, and more by feeling useless, or like a spent force. Spending time in conversation with friends of a younger age group can be very enriching and mutually supportive; it can build a bridge of understanding. For the younger generation, spending time with older people can be a valuable way to learn about life in a previous era, and gain a little wisdom along the way.

"One of the most important friendships of my recent adult life has been with a wonderful woman in her late nineties, who was my neighbor for many years. She has always been an independent thinker and a free spirit. She was a conscientious objector during the war and has always done things in a way that remained true to her ideals. She continued to read one of the more liberal newspapers daily, until her eyesight was no longer able to cope, and was always a lot better informed about what was going on in the world than people half her age. I think her carers found her rather a handful initially as she is a natural rebel, but I always loved her company. She was almost twice my age on paper, but seemed half my age in reality! We could talk about anything and everything. She was never shocked and was extremely wise. I miss her company daily."

Sarah

"I grew up during the war years and there were very few men around. We were all brought up solo, by our mothers; well, everyone's mother really. If you stepped out of line, you were as likely to be told off by a neighbor as your own parent. They were strict times—but there was a lot of freedom, too. My friends and I got into a lot more mischief than we should have done, but mainly we helped each other to make things.

I moved away, so I lost touch; but the older I get, the more I remember those days. I would enjoy meeting some of my childhood friends again."

Robert

"Rose and I met in the late 1940s when we were working on a farm. We were both in our early twenties and were the only girls on the team. We had been given accommodation in a little caravan. There was no running water, and we had to fill the gas lamps every night. It was hard, laboring work, but enormous fun, and it felt as if we spent most of the summer laughing. I had left school at fourteen, during the war years, so I really enjoyed Rose's company because she had been to university and seemed to know so much, but she was very shy. Over the course of the summer, when we had time off, she helped me to feel more confident in the company of those who had been better educated than me, and I think I helped her to gain more confidence socially. We were both quite private people, so we didn't share our innermost thoughts, but I trusted her implicitly. Here we are, sixty years later, still writing to each other. She knows where I began, before I was married and had children."

May

Life happens

The friends we grew up with or enjoyed having fun with when we were younger are not necessarily the ones we will turn to when the going gets tough. Sometimes friends change roles in our lives, depending on circumstances. The one who is quietly patient and sensitive to our needs when we are troubled may also be particularly cautious, and may not join us on our adventures when we are feeling ready to embrace life once again.

It is human nature sometimes to want to distance ourselves from the thing or the person who we associate with a time of pain. Sadly, if the only conversations that we have had with our supportive friend/s are about the trauma of a sad event we want to put behind us, then the very person who helped us to recover may also become a part of the negative memory.

"My partner left me, literally holding the baby, soon after our daughter was born. One of my work friends was absolutely fantastic. She stepped up to help me adjust to the situation and seemed endlessly ready to listen to my woes. I must have been a real pain! She really helped me to think through my options and decide what I was going to do next. Once I got back on my feet I am ashamed to say I did start to feel a bit frustrated by her seriousness and tendency to analyze everything. I am quite a doer and she is definitely more of a thinker. She always finds a reason to say no when my daughter and I are heading off somewhere for the day. We are still good friends, and I am very fond of her—and extremely grateful for her care and support—but I don't see her quite as often as I used to."

Penny

On other occasions, previous life experience can lend understanding to another person's situation and therefore bring us closer. For those facing up to serious illness or even terminal disease, the support of friends is especially precious.

"I had been diagnosed with MS and had retreated within myself. I didn't want to be defined by my illness and didn't want to have to explain why I couldn't go dancing or out for a drink any more. What I hadn't realized was that my friend's mother had had MS, too. He had never mentioned it because his mother hadn't wanted her condition to impact on her children's lives and choices, and he had learnt not to talk about it.

It did have an impact on him, of course, and my friend understood better than I did what the illness was all about. He could so easily have run for the hills when faced with this repeat episode in his life; but he isn't scared by it and has been an incredible support to me over the past few years."

David

Marianne lost her mother far too young. It has left her with an acute awareness of what it feels like to lose a parent, combined with a gift for compassion and practicality that means she is a wonderfully comforting person to have around in a crisis. When she discovered that one of her closest friends was dying, her immediate instinct was to make herself as available as possible to help the family. Over a period of months, without wavering, she helped her friend put her financial affairs in order, drove her to appointments, and spent many hours talking to her when she was too drugged up to respond with anything more than a weak thumbs-up sign. Not everyone could manage to achieve what she did without a qualm, but as she says, the real joy was in the laughter they shared during the penultimate days. The illness could not combat her friend's positivity, and Marianne's indomitable spirit carried the whole family along with her. It was the greatest gift of friendship she could have offered to her friend during her final weeks.

Loss and grief

The joy of friendship in life is connected to the sadness of passing. None of us is immune to the pain of loss or grieving for someone who we have cared about who is no longer around. Sometimes that may mean a relationship break-up, or it may mean a loss of life. In the western world we try to build a wall around ourselves that protects us from any form of suffering, but as every spiritual tradition makes clear, it is through suffering that we grow and develop understanding. Being able to share our thoughts and feelings with others not only helps us to come to terms with our loss, it also keeps alive our shared memories. In grief, people are drawn together. They experience the healing power of supportive love and laughter, as well as tears.

"When friends die, you realize just how unique, precious, and irreplaceable they are. In the midst of a tragedy, from our physical human perspective, the world can feel pretty lonely, empty, and bleak without them. Thankfully, I keep being reminded that separation is an illusion, our spirits never die, and love is eternal. When I attended a funeral service for a dear friend who passed away at the young age of 55, I realized that with loss can come reflection, wisdom, and even motivation. We'd worked as colleagues and also shared baseball, camping, and skiing adventures, together with his wife and friends. He suffered through a long struggle with cancer and complications without complaint, and brought only joy to everyone who knew him. I can only guess that his mission in this lifetime was accomplished. His bright spirit and his wife's great strength will always be inspirational. His passing resonated with me as a reminder that I still have much work to do. When friends die, it's our job to be strong and carry on, but remember to have fun along the way."

Elizabeth Rose, author of *Diamond Lantern*

In being aware of what it is to lose someone, we may also be better prepared for loss, and more attuned to appreciating our friends for themselves, what they bring to us, and how much more fun and enjoyable they make our lives.

Our four-legged friends (and other animals)

Another kind of lifelong friend deserves a very special mention. Our furry, feathered, and fettered friends have offered us companionship and support, and have helped us to survive over centuries.

Those who have spent time working or living with elephants, big cats, gorillas, or other mammals, have no doubt about animals' loyalty to their family group. They look out for one another and take care of their own as far as possible. It may be largely instinct, but there is surely more to it than that. It is incredibly moving to witness animals caring for one another and looking out for each other's needs.

People who have a strong bond with their pets will often agree that their animal friends can recognize changes in their mood and will be protective toward them. Owners will tell stories of their beloved pets offering them comfort or showing signs of happiness or distress that echo whatever they are going through.

While cats, horses, and many other creatures tend to retain their sense of animal superiority, one animal is probably more unquestioningly loyal and devoted than any other; the family dog. Domestic dogs are natural pack animals. They will usually happily accept their place in the family hierarchy and many seem to be able to to tune in to our moods and reflect back to us what is going on, via their own behavior.

"Tigger hated us falling out. She would become very subdued and lie down under the table, but if we hugged, she would jump up and want a hug too! A bit of a challenge sometimes as she was a rather large dog!"

Jane

"A friend of mine had an amazing dog called Frankie. She had the wisest face I have ever seen in an animal and she would protect their baby son as if he was one of her own puppies. Interestingly, other dogs treated her with great respect, too. Like her owner, she was a natural leader of the pack and everyone loved her."

Laura

Pat lived in Zimbabwe and grew up surrounded by animals. She says that one of the strongest bonds she ever witnessed was between two dogs, one of which had been badly injured during a storm. The other dog refused to leave its friend's side for several days, and lasted without food until help arrived.

Many animals form friendship bonds. Here are a few examples:

- Scientists studying whales in the Gulf of St Lawrence have discovered that female humpback whales form bonds that can last for as long as six years. Even though they spend much of the year apart, they seek each other out when they gather again in the open ocean during the summer. The ones that have the most enduring "friendships" give birth to the healthiest calves.

- Female Asian elephants have been found to behave in a similar way to humans. Some form long-lasting bonds with two or three close friends; others act more like social butterflies and can have ten to fifty acquaintances.

- Dolphins, bats, and chimpanzees have been found to form long-standing bonds that could be called friendships. Dolphins recognize and respond to individual calls made by other dolphins, even when they have spent months apart. Bats literally hang out with familiar fellow bats. Chimpanzees are especially friendly, and form protective bonds with animals of other species, too.

Where does friendship stop and survival start? There is an interesting connection and blending between the two. We have a lot to learn from the bonds created in the animal kingdom, which are probably some of the strongest that can be witnessed. Wild animals know better than any other creature that they need to get along with one another in order to survive and thrive.

We need old friends to help us to grow old;
and new friends to help us stay young.

Letty Cottin Pogrebin

5

TELLING IT LIKE IT IS

One of the most beautiful qualities
of true friendship is to understand,
and to be understood.

Seneca (4BCE–AD65)

The importance of honesty

True friends are the ones who lift our spirits
and tell us when we are being wonderful, but
are also not afraid to tell us the truth when
things go askew. They are willing to
risk possible rejection to tell us
something we need to hear.
However, sometimes friends fall
out. One moment the person you
are speaking to is one of your best
friends in the world; the next
moment they say or do
something that makes you
question their judgment, or alters
your perception of who they are. When
we are younger, we may think that a single argument means the end
of a relationship; but with maturity and perseverance, we come to
realize that relationships are more likely to strengthen through
disagreement. A friendship between two people who hide their true
feelings is no friendship at all. The key to resolving differences is to
find a way of communicating that addresses the behavior rather than
attacking the person. It is often the style and tone of language used
that leads to misunderstandings, rather than by the actual words we
say to one another. In any relationship, what we each want more than
anything is to be cared about and to be understood.

Your personal style

Bev James is renowned for her work using personality profiling to help build stronger teams and resolve situations that cause personal conflict in businesses. She explains that although we are complex and unique individuals, we all share four core personality styles that ebb and flow depending on the circumstances. The reasons why we fall out and the ways in which we apologize may differ, depending on which style we feel most comfortable with. Understanding how our personality influences our actions and reactions can help us to understand our friends, and ourselves, much better. The following is based on the profiling method that is central to her work and is explained in her book, *Do it! or Ditch it!*

Driven and decisive

We all know people who are natural go-getters and like to be the leaders of the pack. You will recognize these friends because they are quick to take action when they have an idea or hit a problem. They make fast decisions and hate to fail or feel exploited. They are extremely loyal toward their friends, but may be no-nonsense about losing contact with someone who they feel has taken advantage of them. They will confront you head-on when things go wrong, but are unlikely to hold grudges. Watch what they do, rather than what they say, to show their remorse.

- Best way to tell t how it is: be direct, honest, straightforward, and to the point.
- Most likely to: tell you immediately that they are annoyed and feel taken advantage of. ("I don't care what the reason was. I'm really fed up with you making me late.")

- Best way to resolve a disagreement: focus on a positive outcome. This friend hates being encumbered by detail. ("I understand why you're annoyed. Let's find a way to resolve things and put it behind us.")

Influential and impulsive

Some friends are very sociable and may be the party animals of your group. They love to talk, although their favorite topic of conversation is probably themselves! They tend to be warm and generous people who are extremely focused on their friends when they are with them, and may treat even new acquaintances as if they were close confidants. However, they have a fear of being unpopular, so these friends may also bend with the wind and change social groups quite easily. These friends usually find it easy to apologize because they hate to let you down or feel they might be disliked. The apology will usually be well intentioned, but try not to feel too let down if the same thing happens again.

Best way to tell it how it is: let them speak first, so they will then listen to what you have to say afterwards.

Most likely to: tell you they are sorry, make an exaggerated excuse, and tell you how they are feeling. ("I'm sorry I missed your birthday. I've had the most dreadful week, and then to top it all off, my brother's dog ate my address book.")

Best way to resolve a disagreement: explain why their behavior annoyed you. Reassure them that you still like them, and it's just something that has happened, which you need to discuss. These friends tend to forgive and forget quite quickly.

Steady and sensitive

These friends tend to be very loyal and may be quite conservative. They are fearful of change because it disturbs their sense of security.

They are also very protective of others. Once upset, the wound runs deep and they may find it hard to forgive and forget, although they may never tell you how they are feeling. If you have a disagreement, you will likely need to make amends promptly; otherwise the resentment may fester and you could lose a friend.

Best way to tell it how it is: focus on feelings, be sincere, and offer practical reassurance.

Most likely to: check whether you are all right, rather than tell you that they are upset. ("Are you okay? Would you like a cup of tea?")

Best way to resolve a disagreement: focus on their feelings and reassure them that it won't happen again.

Cautious and compliant

These are the friends who will go on the defensive if criticized, even if they are in the wrong, and they may overanalyze a situation, too. They may drop you a little note to apologize and explain, rather than picking up the phone to talk about things. They are also the people who can keep their true feelings hidden and may sometimes put up with a lot in order to avoid the discomfort of conflict.

Best way to tell it how it is: go over things in enough detail to make sure your friend is feeling listened to and understood.

Most likely to: overanalyze and try to justify their actions by giving you a logical explanation in some detail. ("I would normally have been on time, but the council re-routed the traffic this morning.")

Best way to resolve a disagreement: focus on the essential facts but avoid getting drawn into the detail.

Of course, as Bev James explains, most of us are a mix of two or more of these core traits, and the intensity of our reactions alters depending on circumstances. We may choose to behave differently, depending on our situation and what is expected of us. However, in general, if we can learn to see things from our friend's point of view, and talk to them in a style that they prefer when they are under pressure, we are less likely to fall out in the first place—and if we do, we will be quicker to forgive and forget.

> May the roof above our heads never fall in, and may we friends below never fall out.
>
> **Irish saying**

Enduring friendships

Sharing adventures, holidays, and new experiences is that stuff that friendships are made of. However, it is often during the tough times that we discover whether our friendships will endure. When a friend is in crisis, most of us will have a natural tendency to reach out in support. Suddenly, past slights are forgotten. Our compassion for the other person takes over and instantly we are in the zone and ready to help.

Just as a parent will gradually encourage a child to stand on their own two feet, so too a friend may need encouragement to let go of their pain and start to walk again. Sometimes people become stuck in a cycle of destructive thinking or victim behavior, and as a friend you become an unwitting part of the pattern. Before you know it, you are thinking more about their problem than they are themselves. If that happens, it may be necessary to toughen up and tell your friend how you feel. Don't panic if they become snappy, that is human nature and the mood will pass.

Asking for support

We all have times when it feels as if friendly support is one-way traffic, from you to someone else. This may be fine for a while, until something serious happens and a yawning gap appears where the mutual support was expected to be. Some people expect their friends to know instinctively when something is amiss in their lives. These people may feel affronted when their friends don't ask the right questions, or are distracted and don't follow through with support at the right moment. But is that really fair? Our friends are not responsible for our welfare; we are. One of the hardest things for some people to learn is to make their needs known and to ask others for what they would like. For others, it is the easiest thing in the world to say, "Please could you help me? I don't think I can achieve this on my own."

Simple dos and don'ts to help safeguard your friendships:

- Don't tell boyfriends/mothers/children/husbands/wives/anyone else embarrassing stories about friends.
- And while we're on that subject, don't post pictures or stories about friends on Facebook, either.
- If you've arranged to meet, don't be late. (Well, ten minutes is okay, but a half-hour is just rude, no matter how much they care about you.)
- Don't go off in a huff if someone says something you disagree with. Stay and talk it over face to face; you can take it.
- Do pay friends back without having to be asked, if you said you'd go halves for a night out.
- Do give back the best sweater/favorite book/lawnmower a friend lent you, and try to make sure it hasn't been stretched/creased/broken.
- If you miss your friends when they're not around, chances are they're missing you, too, so drop them a line to say hello.
- Do remember friends' birthdays, at least by sending a card.
- Say thank you. No one likes to be taken for granted.
- Do keep secrets forever—even if you fall out—and trust your friends will keep yours, too.

The wisdom of the Buddha

Be aware of four enemies disguised as friends: the taker, the talker, the flatterer, and the reckless companion.

The Buddha

In her blog "The Buddha's advice to lay people" Lynn J. Kelly introduces the idea of "wholesome companions." This is not about being as wholesome as apple pie, but about being a whole friend; someone who is fully present in the friendship. Wholesome friends are the ones who bring out the best in you; they promote friendships of mutual respect and understanding. You may be inspired by them or want to emulate them. A wholesome friend is honest with you and helps to keep you on track.

Buddhist wisdom advises us to be wary of:

- The taker, who asks for a lot while giving little and tends to put their own needs first.
- The talker, who is all talk and no action and tends to make promises that they can't keep.
- The flatterer, who praises you to your face, but talks about you behind your back.
- The reckless companion, who encourages you to give in to your weaker impulses, such as taking that extra drink/cake/cigarette, and "to heck with the gym membership."

Buddhist wisdom advises us to seek out:

- The helper, who protects you and offers you help and refuge when you are under threat or pressure.
- The enduring friend, who will stick with you through a crisis and can be trusted to stand by you.
- The mentor, who keeps you focused on your goals and is honest with you, telling you what you need to hear.
- The compassionate friend who celebrates your good fortune without envy, and praises you to others.

Of course, the chances are that we each show a mix of all these traits at some time or another, but trying consistently to show one another wisdom, patience, honesty, and compassion can only build stronger friendships and bring us closer together.

Saying goodbye to a friendship

We don't always behave well in life. Sometimes we do things we regret, and sometimes we lose good friends in the process. Not all friendships are forever, and it can be hard to let go of someone who has shared an important part of your life, but we don't necessarily grow and change in the same way as our friends. Sometimes we discover that we no longer have anything in common. Letting go of a friendship can be painful, especially if there are differing expectations on both sides.

Mark and Rory had been friends for years. They had been workmates and flatmates and knew each other well. When Rory's wife left him, he turned to Mark for support. He used to drop round for a beer or to talk; sometimes staying for hours. Mark put him up while his divorce and house sale went through. Rory struggled with his grief but gradually got himself back on his feet. He started to socialize more often and moved job too.

When Mark was made redundant from his job, he found it tough, emotionally and financially, but little support was forthcoming from Rory. His old friend would still drop round but now told Mark all about his new girlfriends, how much money he was earning, and the holidays he had planned. His lack of sensitivity to Mark's situation began to wear Mark down. Mark felt annoyed, and reached a point where he just didn't want to speak to Rory any more. In retrospect, he wishes he'd had it out with Rory, "And told him what a self-absorbed so-and-so he had become. Instead," he says, "I just gradually cooled the friendship. He was a fun guy, and I still miss his company sometimes, but the truth is I felt let down and I expected more from one of my best mates. I just didn't want to be in contact any more."

The art of forgiveness

Friends who fall out can find it hard to forgive one another. The silence between them may become as solid and impenetrable as a brick wall. Over time the details of the disagreement either become blurred and forgotten, or else become larger than life and exaggerated. Where once there was lightness there is now heaviness and anger, or indifference. The irony is that disagreements expend energy and increase negative thoughts—feelings that hurt us more than they do the other person. The weight of the anger, jealousy, hurt, or disappointment chips away at our capacity for happiness and constrains our movements. "I can't go to see friend X because ex-friend Y is friends with them, too." "I don't go there any more because I know X often goes there." In reality, roots of the disagreement usually lie with both or all involved, but moving beyond the problem to an apology is easier for some than for others.

"A brief conversation I had many years ago has proven to have lasting positive effects. I was discussing with a work friend a wrangle I was in with a family member. She listened patiently, watching my expressions as well as hearing my words. When I finished, she allowed for a pause and a breath. She looked at me directly and asked, "Can you find any love in the relationship?" I had to think for a minute, because this question forced me off the self-righteous track I was on. Finally, I took a breath and said, "Yes. There is love in this relationship." She said, "Then go with the love. Just go with the love." This conversation was like a seed planted in my heart. Every time I recall it and make use of it, it grows. Over time, it has created a habit; to seek out the love element in every situation, especially when I feel ensnared."

Lynn J. Kelly, Buddhist teacher

In friendship, as in so many things in life, we reach a truer point of understanding when we manage to get out of our own way. It is rare that a friend actually means us harm. Usually they are just doing the best they can with the tools of life that they have available.

Walking with a friend in the dark is better than walking alone in the light.

Helen Keller (1880–1968)

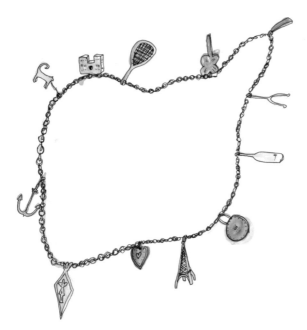

6

WORKING
FRIENDSHIPS

No man is an island, entire of
itself; every man is a piece of the
continent, a part of the main.

John Donne (1572–1631)

Workplace bonds

Many of us spend more hours with our colleagues than with any other person in our life, so it is not surprising that some of our strongest and most lasting friendships develop through our work. We may show more consideration for our colleagues than we do for our own family, and more tolerance for their weaknesses. The people we work with see our vulnerabilities at close hand, as well as our strengths, and they see how we deal with them, too. Bonds strengthen when problems are faced together, and when they are overcome as a team. Friendships forged at work make the day go faster, and things tend to get done more quickly. Those people who have made friends at work are statistically more likely to say that they enjoy their job and are less likely to be disruptive or to leave. Many people who are starting out create bonds of friendship in the early stages of their career that last for the rest of their lives.

The work/friendship dynamic

Working friendships have particular challenges. Closeness can dissipate or may change form when roles change or hard decisions have to be made. Resentments can occur when a work-focused decision has to take precedence over the needs of a friendship.

Marie is a life coach and student mentor who gives talks to students, helping them to prepare for job applications and employment. She always stresses the importance of respecting, and getting along with, colleagues in the workplace, at every level. "What some people tend to forget," she says, "is that those who are your contemporaries today will be colleagues and competitors for many years going forward. No matter how high you fly, you will meet your contemporaries again in many situations—and also when you come back down—so I always say to people: 'Play nicely; the working relationships you make early on may influence areas of your working life over a very long time.' "

The friendly boss

Fortunately, the era of the autocratic boss, who sits at the top of the hierarchy wielding their power, seems to be on the wane. Flat business structures, informal job titles, and casual work attire in many young businesses lay the ground for a new kind of leader; one who has the courage to be true to themselves and who has the strength of character to nurture and encourage rather than shout and dictate to the team. Nice is "in." It's official, people enjoy working, and are more efficient and productive, when they are in a pleasant working environment!

Help—I am the boss!

One of the hardest transition points at work is having to adjust from being one of the team to being the boss. Even those who are natural-born leaders can suffer nervous moments when they are promoted to lead the pack rather than be a part of it. It can be lonely at the top—and it can be lonely at the head of the meeting-room table, too. Trying to lead work colleagues who are also your friends can be challenging; that's why so many people leave the company they are with and move elsewhere to gain promotion.

Tips for maintaining your workplace friendships when you're asked to take the lead:

- Remain natural. Treat everyone with the same courtesy and respect you have always done, and be upfront and open in your discussions.
- Make your own decisions. Listen to what people have to say, but resist the temptation to defer, or try to please everyone.
- Keep your own counsel. Don't be tempted to confide in your friends and tell them about confidential business.
- Take time to gather your thoughts so you know what you are going to say. Try not to talk too much and keep things simple.
- Plan ahead. Be prepared to stay ahead of the game.
- Keep personal loyalties and business priorities separate in your new role.
- Be a team player. Winning respect is easy when you respect and champion the skills and achievements of your team.
- Find a mentor who can help you to find your way.
- Don't expect to maintain all your friendships. If some people choose to drift away, try to be philosophical and let them go. It is about them, not you.

No doubt some of the people who you previously thought of as friends may resist the idea of you being promoted above them, but take a deep breath and let it go. A career is likely to last for twenty years or more. Focus on the long game. There will always be grumblers on the team, but differences of opinion don't need to become personal.

Leaving the fold

Ironically, in an office-based or standard work environment, it may not be until you leave your place of work that relationships strengthen. You may like your colleagues but not know them all that well, but when you announce that you are leaving for pastures new, you may suddenly find that you become a confidant for those who will still be there when you have gone. There are several reasons for this:

You are leaving so it's safe to confide in you. You understand the culture and the past, and you have no reason to tell anyone what is being said.

Others may be planning to leave, too, and since you're going, they feel they can talk to you about their plans.

You are on neutral ground so people feel it's safe to discuss their plans for their role within their present company.

There is a sense of uncertainty surrounding the future. No one knows who will be taking your place, whereas you are a known entity.

Going it alone

More people than ever before are choosing to set up in business for themselves, but to be a success, especially as a one-man or one-woman band, it is important to be a team player. Business associates may also become friends; they are the people who you can rely upon to help make things happen.

Ask yourself some pertinent questions:

- Which of your friends are networkers? These are the people who know who's who, what's what, and who might need your services.
- Who are the doers? You need people on your side who can be relied upon to help you to deliver a good job on time.
- Some friends will be influencers. We all know people who can open doors and know how and when to increase your profile.
- Are you comfortable delegating? Those who reach the greatest heights also value the skills of others.
- Are you reliable? Friends will remain friends only if they can count on each other to do what they say they will, when they say they will do it.

Workplace friendships may develop quite quickly, although some are friendships of convenience and may be less likely to survive the passing of time. It may be wise to remember that not everyone you speak to can keep a confidence. Workplace gossip is the in-house entertainment; it travels fast, and can reach high places. If something is going on in your private life that you would rather keep private, it may be worth thinking twice before talking about it at work—and be very, very careful about what you share on your Facebook or other pages!

"I would never have expected to become friends with my clients when I started out, but it has been an unexpected bonus to discover that the bonds we have been building through our work have developed a life beyond the deadlines. My professional friendships are some of my most precious, because they are built on mutual respect as well as on liking one another."

Caroline

"I really look forward to meeting up with my former colleagues. Four of us get together every six months or so. Funnily enough, we still fall back into our old roles slightly, even though we have all moved on, grown up, and done many new things with our lives."

Erin

"The best part of my job is seeing the people I work with every day. We get the job done and we have great laughs at the same time. We are a great team.

Nicky

None of us is as smart as all of us.

Kenneth Blanchard

7

LOVE AND FRIENDSHIP

I love you, not only for what you are, but for what I am when I am with you ... perhaps that is what being a friend means after all.

Roy Croft (c.1905–1980)

Love, respect, acceptance

Love and friendship go hand in hand. We hold great love in our hearts for our dearest friends and will go out of our way for them when they are in trouble or in need of our support. Sometimes just being there is all that is needed to show someone how much we care. Love is about accepting someone as they truly are, faults and all, rather than expecting them to be someone else or trying to get them to change. We tend to love our friends *because* of their imperfections, rather than in spite of them.

Ask a married couple who have been together for decades what has kept them together all these years and they are likely to use words such as "compromise," "respect," "kindness," "acceptance," and "friendship." Ask them whether they love one another and most will answer with an unqualified, "Yes," although they will probably acknowledge that it hasn't been plain sailing and there have been challenges along the way.

> "Friendship is the glue that keeps things together when the going gets tough. I must admit, there have been a few times when I have wanted to walk out of the door, and there was also a time when I was very tempted to stray for a moment. But when it came right down to it, he is my best friend. I don't think I could ever do anything that would cause him pain or would hurt him. We have been through too much together."
>
> **Claire**

Better together

Erich Fromm, the German psychologist and social philosopher, and author of *The Art of Loving*, saw the state of loving as beginning with the ability to care for and respect oneself. He saw love not as a separate state in which two people are devoted only to one another and exist in isolation from the rest of humankind, but as an extension of the love we show to one another universally. He believed that in a loving relationship two individuals should be capable of feeling responsibility for each other and showing each other care and respect, taking the time truly to know one another,

and they should maintain the ability to show loving kindness to others as well. Such a solid foundation takes time to build, and friendship has an

important part to play. We are happiest when our relationships combine both love and friendship, attraction and familiarity, adventure and peace, when we are better together than we are alone.

"I'm a better person when I'm with Steph.
She challenges my cynicism and makes me see the good in people."

Mike

"Mike is my best friend. He encourages me to be braver and to try new things. And I feel safe enough to have a go because I know he will look out for me."

Stephanie

Understanding love and friendship

Where does friendship end and love begin? What is the difference between love and attraction, and why does friendship so often seem to come either before or after we have fallen madly in love? Why is it so hard for love and friendship to live side by side?

These are universal questions and the answers are not straightforward. In some societies it is still unacceptable for men and women to socialize. The same was true in western societies in earlier centuries. When men and women are living parallel lives, it can be harder to get to know one another. No wonder our elders used to choose our partners, and marriages of convenience were the norm. These days men and women are more usually free to make their own choices—and their own mistakes!

However, there is confusion, too. Falling in love and being overwhelmingly attracted to someone sometimes seems to be the only aim. Nothing less will do. It is heady stuff and can be a powerful force, changing lives in an instant. But intensity of emotion changes form over time. When passion starts to cool, the solid foundation of friendship helps to ensure that a relationship builds and survives over time.

In ancient times, friendship and kinship were taken extremely seriously. The old adage, "Keep your friends close, but your enemies closer," was important. Monarchs and leaders would offer their children in marriage as the ultimate token of alliance. Beads, pictures, gifts, animals, land, and other material treasures would form the bride's dowry. Marriage was far from being sentimental or about love; it was for convenience. Unsurprisingly romantic relationships became idealized; they were seen as an escape route away from neglect, boredom, or worse. It is human nature to keep trying to find the perfect partner.

Plato was one of the earliest philosophers to try to define the different states of friendship, love, and attachment. He spoke of the transformation from the state of Vulgar Eros (Earthly love,) which was physical attraction for its own sake, to Divine Eros (Platonic love)—a state of mind in which you are inspired by love to reach a more spiritual plane and seek Divine love. These days Platonic love is thought of as romantic, non-sexual, and the search for perfection. Can there be room for true friendship in such an idealized relationship?

"I was a bit of an idealist when I was younger. I never got involved with guys who were my good friends. I fell slightly in love with each of them at some point or another, because they were all lovely, fun people, and still are. But I didn't want to take the risk of losing their friendship if it all went wrong. Perhaps it was my conservative upbringing. I probably missed out on a lot of fun over the years! But for me, if the friendship was more valuable than the attraction, then it obviously wasn't worth the risk."

Teri

"I used to spend a fortune on my would-be girlfriends—dinner, theater, gifts, taxis home, you name it. They used to tell me their troubles and say I was a great friend—and then fall for a guy who didn't do any of those things! To top it off, they would complain that Mr Wrong didn't do this, didn't do that—remember birthdays, care about them, etc etc. What is all that about? Eventually I realized that I was playing a role. My current girlfriend is also my best friend. I can be myself with her and she accepts me for who I am."

George

"I spent most of my twenties and thirties in a permanent state of heartbreak. I always seemed to be getting hurt and falling for the wrong guys. It took me a while to wake up to the fact that I was as guilty as they were of showing myself a lack of love and care. I was chasing thrills and expecting love. It doesn't work like that. It took a motorcycle accident to wake me up to what was important in life. It wasn't the guy I was madly in love with who supported me through rehab; it was one of my oldest and dearest friends. His humor, strength, and encouragement saw me through. 'Reader, I married him!' as they say."

Anne

Clicking and connecting

These days people are seeking love and choosing friends in many different ways—online, via mobile phone, by tweeting, or just plain old-fashioned talking—but it can be hard to take the time to get to know people when romance and sex are clearly on the agenda. For those who are uncertain, changing the focus from love to friendship can be a way of testing the water, slowing things down, showing respect for one another, and being sure.

Falling in love, and the powerful feelings that it brings with it, is a gift to be savored, but the love and friendship that we experience along the way makes us who we are. That's what helps us to recognize when something truly special has happened, and when we have met someone whom we want to make a permanent part of our lives.

Sometimes, when people get involved in a new relationship, they draw back from spending time with their friends. It's not deliberate, but the new boyfriend or girlfriend suddenly becomes all-consuming and center stage. However, with a few more years' experience and wisdom, hopefully we no longer make that mistake. Getting together with friends can be a useful way of finding out whether a relationship is likely to be right in the long run, especially as we usually turn to our friends for support when things don't turn out quite as planned. Our friends show their love by wanting to protect us, even if we don't always want to listen to what they have to say.

Ways in which to express our love and friendship:
- Acceptance: we are disappointed by others when they don't live up to our expectations, but if we accept people for who they are, we can never be disappointed by them, and then they will surpass our expectations.

- Being there: one of the key elements of being a good friend is just showing up. Sometimes, all our friends need is for us to be there for them and offer support, and we need them to be there for us, too

- Resilience: friendships that have weathered tough times will transform into something more lasting and resistant. Knowing that a friend has the resilience to cope when life gets difficult makes us value them even more, and helps us to develop our own resilience.

- Listening: everyone needs an agony aunt. Friends who give their time, and try to listen to our troubles without judgment, are worth their weight in gold. Respecting their time, and making sure that we don't weigh them down with our difficulties, is a way to repay that kindness. Friendship that becomes a duty is no friendship at all.

- Trust: the foundation stone of friendship is trust. Once betrayed, it can never be regained. Friends who offer one another trust do it not just for a moment; it is an enduring pact that lasts indefinitely.

- Humor: we love our friends' quirky ways, their differences, and their uniqueness. Shared jokes and humor are a shortcut to mutual understanding that binds us together in an intimate and personal way. Humor reminds us of the essence that connects us and keeps us laughing. It reminds us of how much we enjoy being together, and all the things we share.

Letting go

We change over time, and other people change, too. There are times in life when we need to let go of a past love or friendship, even though on some level our feelings for that person may remain strong. Sometimes, who we have been, or what we have had in the past, can no longer continue into the future.

Love is not a finite pot to be filled, it is an infinite and unending state of being. It is not a matter of no longer loving one person because of our love for someone else. It is a matter of choosing what feels right in life and making the sometimes hard decisions that lead to greater happiness, personal growth, and joy, for all involved.

Sometimes when we choose to step away from our past, we choose to step away from valued friends as well. When loyalties split or trust is shattered, the ripples affect others, and they too find that choices need to be made.

If you are at a time in your life when it feels as if friends have abandoned you, it can be helpful to remember that time really is a great healer, and things may change a little further down the line. It may also help to reach out to new friends.

The greatest joy of friendship is that, in our hearts, we always have room for more.

Friendship is certainly the finest balm for the pangs of disappointed love.

Jane Austen (1775–1817)

8

I'VE GOT TO BE ME, YOU'VE GOT TO BE YOU

I don't need a friend who changes when I change, and nods when I nod; my shadow does that much better.

Plutarch (46–c.AD120)

Valuing differences

The true joy of friendship lies in our sense of being understood, loved, and accepted for who we are, and in being trusted with another person's thoughts and dreams. Friends value each other for their differences as well as their similarities. We love our friends for being uniquely themselves.

Friendship is a two-way track

The quality of our friendships is closely linked to our sense of self; our goals, ambitions, dreams, and hopes for the future. Our friends influence our attitudes and potential for success and happiness, and we influence them in the same way.

When we reach the big milestones in our lives, friends reach out to one another for support and encouragement, to share in the joy or the sadness of the moment. Sometimes, our paths diverge, and sometimes friendships fade, but whatever happens, we will have shared important times in our lives. Our friends have a lasting impact on us; they have helped to shape the choices we have made in the past, and will influence the ones we make about the future.

Friendship is a two-way track. It is a responsibility, but it is never an obligation.

Have you ever been to a school or college reunion? Meeting long-lost friends and acquaintances again can be fascinating, and a wonderful way of reconnecting with people you thought had been lost to your life forever. However, the experience can be emotionally disruptive, too. To misquote L.P. Hartley, "The past is a foreign country—we did things differently there." People from our past may remind us of events or aspects of ourselves that we had forgotten about. We all edit our memories over time.

We never stop changing

When we are young, we seek friends who seem similar to ourselves. By emulating each other and trying on opinions and attitudes for size, we learn a lot about ourselves; where the similarities lie, and how the points of difference matter. As we get older, the differences become as interesting as the similarities. We want to feel comfortable with our friends, but we don't need them to be the same as us. We value their individuality as well as their predictability. We love the fact that our friends know how we think, and we understand what makes them laugh, but we also want to hear their opinions and learn their take on things. Seeing the world through another person's eyes can help us to make sense of ourselves, and to see things in new and interesting ways.

The truth is we never stop evolving and growing. The more enquiring we are, the more enriched and interesting life becomes. Sometimes we need to let go of our image of our past self in order to become who we might truly be. Into those times may step new friends who help us to evolve and to see life in a new way. The joy of friendship is limitless, and all it takes to begin to make friends is a smile, and the first "Hello."

A friend is someone who knows all about you,
and still loves you.

Elbert Hubbard (1856–1915)

Afterword

In honor of friends and friendship

You are my friend. You hold a special place in my heart.

You have made me laugh more times than I can remember, in the knowing way that only a friend can. Your company makes me happy. Seeing you lifts my spirit and meeting up is a joy because you understand who I truly am. You are ready to celebrate the fun, adventure, and madness of life with me at a moment's notice. You comfort me when I am upset and you lift my spirits when I feel down. There are times when you see the best in me when I can only see the bad. You have listened to me when I have faced heartbreak and you have been there to celebrate my joys.

You forgive me when I upset you or let you down. You know the secrets of my youth and I trust you with those memories. You understand my crazy hopes for the future. Thank you for the part you have played in my life so far. You make my world a better place.

Thank you for the warmth and joy of your friendship.

Credits

Page 29. Historical facts provided by Jaci Twidwell, Hallmark spokesperson, Hallmark Inc, USA.
Quotation from: Edgar A. Guest, 'A Friend's Greeting', *Collected Verse of Edgar Guest*, (Buccaneer Books, 1976).

Page 37. Quotation © David Pitonyak, 'The importance of belonging: a report on men and friendship in the 21st century', (Chivas Regal, 2012).

Page 80. Quotation © Elizabeth Rose, *Diamond Lantern: Waking up to who you really are* www.diamondlantern.com. Reproduced with permission.

Pages 87-90. Adapted with permission from Bev James's descriptions of the DISC personality styles in *Do It or Ditch It!* (Virgin, 2011.) The DISC styles are more usually listed as: Dominant, Influencing, Steady, Compliant. DISC is an established tool used in personality profiling. A free online assessment can be taken at www.bevjames.com

Page 99. Quotation © Lynn Kelly, 'The Buddha's advice to lay people' www.buddhasadvice.wordpress.com. Reproduced with permission.

Index

Acknowledgments

This book is written in gratitude to my friends and in honor of friendship. There are many who have helped me with ideas and thoughts for the content, whose names have been changed at their request. Particular love and thanks go to: Veron Lien, Jo and Hannah Burgess, Jane Colston, Sue Hook, Louise Hopkins, Bev James, Sue Lanson, Annette Peppis, Sharee Ryan, Tina Volkmann, Pat Watson, and Kolly.

Enormous thanks to the team at Cico, especially commissioning editor Lauren Mulholland for her creativity and patience, Marion Paull for her skilled editing, Penny Craig for making it all happen, and Cindy Richards, who is simply brilliant. I am immensely grateful, too, to designer Emily Breen and illustrator Amy Louise Evans, whose skills and talent have brought the content to life. Thank you also to Lynn Kelly and Elizabeth Rose for sharing the content of their excellent blogs and to Bev James for being so inspiring.